THE FASHION ICONS

HERMÈS

Alison James

sona
BOOKS

© Danann Media Publishing Limited 2024

First Published Danann Media Publishing Limited 2024

WARNING: For private domestic use only, any unauthorised Copying, hiring, lending or public performance of this book is illegal.

CAT NO: SON0592

Photography courtesy of

Getty images; Alamy; Other images Wiki Commons

Book design Darren Grice at Ctrl-d
Proof reader Finn O'Neill

All rights reserved. No Part of this title may be reproduced or transmitted in any material form (including photocopying or storing it in any medium by electronic means and whether or not transiently or incidentally to some other use of this publication) without the written permission of the copyright owner, except in accordance with the provisions of the Copyright, Designs and Patents Act 1988. Applications for the copyright owner's written permission should be addressed to the publisher.

This is an independent publication and it is unofficial and unauthorised and as such has no connection with Hermès or any other organisation connected in any way whatsoever with Hermès featured in the book.

Made in EU.

ISBN: 978-1-915343-48-2

CONTENTS

INTRODUCTION	8
A BRAND IS BORN	10
THE HERMÈS FAMILY TREE	14
THE NEXT GENERATION	16
EMILE'S TREASURES	32
DAWN OF THE DUMAS DYNASTY	34
LE SCARF	42
JEAN LOUIS AND HIS LEGACY	48
MOST WANTED BIRKIN BAGS	62
FAMILY VALUES	66
HERMÈS BY NUMBERS	74
READY-TO-WEAR CREATIVE DESIGN	76
ICONIC HERMÈS	134
POST SCRIPT	140

INTRODUCTION

'We don't have a policy of image, we have a policy of product'
Jean Louis Dumas, great-great-grandson of Thierry Hermès, founder of the House of Hermès, and Chairman and Artistic Director of the brand from 1978 to 2006

Hermès... the name itself is a work of art and its proper pronunciation must often be taught. 'Air-mez'—as in the messenger god with winged sandals. Founded in Paris as a harness workshop in 1837 by Thierry Hermès, the original intent was to serve the needs of European nobility by providing them with equestrian, leather goods of the highest quality. While exquisite leather work is still very much what Hermès is about, the house has evolved over the years into a family-run business that beats at the very heart of Parisian high fashion. Though Hermès is grouped with other high-end brands, it hovers ineffably higher, apart, and not only because it is more costly and exclusive. Dumas himself dismissed the term 'luxury', disliking its arrogance, its hints of decadence and ostentation. He preferred the word 'refinement' and intrinsic to this is what Hermès refuses to do. It does not boast, does not use celebrities in advertising, does not license its name, does not let imperfect work leave the atelier, does not get its noble head turned by trends. What it does do—Dumas's 'policy of product'— is to create items made from the most beautiful materials on earth, each so intelligently designed and deeply well-made they transcend fashion. As Hermès continues to produce sartorial perfection in myriad forms, we take a look back at the brand's evolution while wondering at its creations, exquisite craftsmanship and iconic designs.

INTRODUCTION 9

A BRAND IS BORN

'Since 1837, every Hermès saddle has been hand-made by a single craftsmen, then specially configured for its rider and horse under the guidance of our saddle expert'

The Hermès website

Hermès of Paris... It is known the world over for its place at the very pinnacle of iconic, uber luxurious, inherently stylish yet understated French chic. The label is Parisian to its core. Strictly speaking, however, Hermès has its roots in Germany. Thierry Hermès, its founder, was born in the city of Krefeld some eight km from the river Rhine. His ancestors were Huguenots (French protestants) who were persecuted under the reigns of Catholic French Kings Louis XV and Louis XIV which led them to flee to the Rhineland area of Germany where they could live in peace. On January 10 1801 baby Thierry was born, the last of six children, to his French immigrant father, Thierry Hermès, and German mother, Agnese Kuenen. By this time, the area had been conquered by Napoleon Bonaparte and in 1797, had become a French territory. The Hermès family ran a silk business on Konigstrasse in the centre of Krefeld. The city had a long history of textile manufacturing and was known as the *'stadt of samt und seidenstadt'* – or *'city of silk and velvet'* in English – with Krefeld's weavers supplying velvet, brocade and silk to many nations. According to some sources, Thierry's parents also ran a hotel which may have been located next to their small factory.

In January 1814, Napoleon was defeated and the region reverted back to its Germanic roots with Krefeld becoming part of Prussia. Life became difficult

ABOVE: Thierry Hermès,
OPP PAGE LEFT: Silk loom as used in Krefeld in the 1800s
OPP PAGE RIGHT: Pont Audemer by Frank Myers Boggs

A BRAND IS BORN

for la famille Hermès. By the age of 17, young Thierry had lost both parents to consumption and, now an orphan, he decided to relocate to Normandy in northern France – where his father's ancestors had hailed from. He settled in Pont Audemer, a small town located between Deauville and Rouen, some 160km north west from Paris. Known as the 'Venice of Normandy' and located on the Risle, a river with many channels, Port Audemer made an ideal base for the leather industry as water was so plentiful. In addition to his knowledge of textiles, Thierry learned the skills of handling leather and was employed by the Pleumer family who owned a successful *'sellier-harnacheur'* or leather production company.

In April 1828 he married local girl, Christine Pierrat. Nine years later and now an artisan of exceptional quality, Thierry, Christine and their six-year-old son, Charles Emile, relocated to to Paris. There were over 70,000 horses in the French capital at the time and Thierry saw a gap in the market for well-made and stylish bridles, carriage fittings and harnesses. The first original Hermès store opened on la Rue Rasse du Rempert in the ninth arrondissement, a neighbourhood then known as 'Grand Boulevards'. Hermès quickly became popular with high-end, carriage businesses and French nobility, including Eugenie, the wife of Emperor Napoleon III. Thierry vowed from the very beginning that Hermès would always be known for the quality of its materials and skill of its artisans and the house quickly garnered a reputation for elegantly understated and well-made tack. Thierry became famous for his innovative and extremely strong saddle stitch. This unique invention was – and still is - made by hand with two needles and two threads of waxed linen, sewed in opposing directions. The genius thought behind it being that if one row of stitches broke or gave way, the other row

THE FASHION ICONS HERMÈS

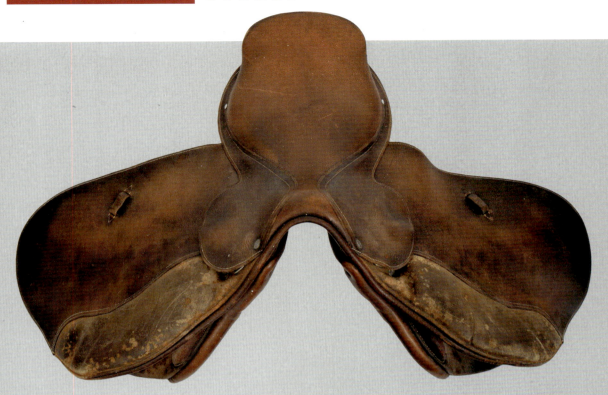

would ensure the item still held together. It is fascinating to note that this 'double stitch' method continues to be employed in the manufacture of every Hermès handbag to this day. Thierry Hermès went on to win awards for his innovations, including several medals at the Exposition Universelle in 1855, and first prize at the 1867 World's Fair in Paris for outstanding technical ability, craftsmanship and design.

Son and heir, Charles-Emile, started working for the family firm in 1859, and like his father was dedicated to ensuring that Hermès' goods were of the finest quality. Charles-Emile took over the reins when Thierry passed away on his 77th birthday in January 1878. By this time, Hermès' reputation was starting to spread across the world, attracting customers from the rest of Europe, Russia, the USA and parts of Asia. The company was expanding at a rate that larger premises were required. This move was hastened by the fact that the visionary who was Baron Hausmann, under the guidance of the Emperor Napoleon III, wished to modernise the Parisian landscape by building large and geometric Avenues. The Rue Basse du Rempart where the Hermès store was located would be demolished in the process. With the help of an eviction payment from the Prefect de Seine, Charles Emile was able to rent a much larger space on the prestigious Rue du Faubourg Saint-Honore where Hermès HQ is still located today. La Maison expanded its range as a result. Between 1880 and 1900, it started making and selling bespoke saddlery, also the "Haut à Courroies" bag, which was created for riders to carry their saddles in.

Until his retirement in 1902, Charles Emile worked with his two sons, Adolphe and Emile after which, les Freres Hermès took over. It was during their joint tenure that Hermès of Paris truly began to come into its own...

ABOVE: Vintage Hermès saddle
RIGHT: Hermès saddle being constructed

A BRAND IS BORN 13

HERMÈS FAMILY TREE

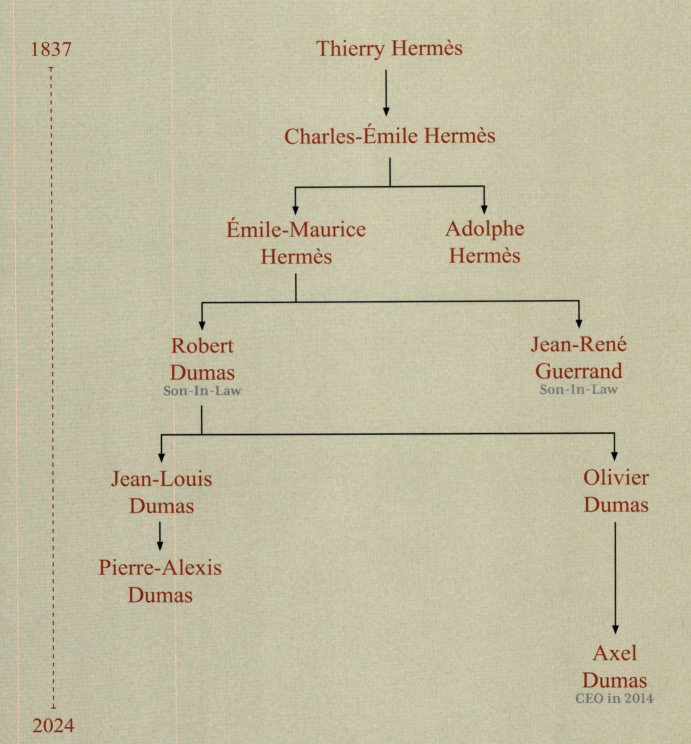

THE HERMÈS FAMILY TREE

THE FASHION ICONS   HERMÈS

THE NEXT GENERATION

'Leather, sport, and a tradition of refined elegance'
Emile-Maurice Hermès describing the company

Following Charles-Émile Hermès's retirement in 1902, sons Adolphe and Émile-Maurice (known as Emile) took over the leadership, temporarily renaming the company Hermès Frères. They were peerless in their field, adding Czar Nicholas II of Russia to their client list, along with other Europen royals and well-to-do riders from around the world. By 1914, the company employed 80 saddle-makers and craftsmen. However, the age of the motorcar had dawned which inevitably meant the decline of horsepower. Cautious elder sibling Adolphe felt the company could not survive as the combustion engine took over but the more adventurous and visionary Émile regarded it as an opportunity. He saw Hermès racing into the age of the automobile alongside motoring vehicles, which would no doubt require leather accessories. Even before the turn of the century he had proved himself to be a man of vision combined with impressive entrepreneurial skills. In 1898 aged 27, he set out for Tsarist Russia – having bought himself a fur-trimmed overcoat – with a notepad full of addresses of the influential people he should meet. He also left with a massive leather trunk which contained miniature models of Hermès' tack to show to potential customers. On Emile's return to Paris, it was said craftsmen worked for months to complete all the orders he had gathered.

It was on another trip some years later that Emile's genius came to the fore. During a visit to North America during the First World War in his capacity as an army officer, he met car manufacturing magnet, Henry Ford, who, at the time, was running the best factories in the world. Then on a visit over the border to Canada, he was inspired by a very simple idea

ABOVE: Charles-Émile Hermès
RIGHT: Émile-Maurice Hermès

THE FASHION ICONS   HERMÈS

that was to revolutionise the House of Hermès and – in the process – the fashion industry as a whole. He became fascinated by the 'close-all' opening-and-closing device on the hood of a military car – the forerunner of the zip or zipper fastening. The zipper opened and closed in a flash, and Emile saw that it would be the perfect mechanism with which to secure a purse or jacket. In 1922, Emile obtained the exclusive rights to this fastening which was initially known as the Hermès Fastener. Émile negotiated a two-year European patent on the zipper. The fastener would go on to change the fashion and clothing industries with Hermès manufacturing the first ever leather jacket with zip fastening in 1918 for the future Duke of Windsor, then Prince of Wales. The Hermès workrooms became so expert in their manipulation of the zip that other companies, including Coco Chanel's, came to learn from them.

In 1919, Emile bought his brother out of the company. While Hermès would continue to produce their heritage equestrian ware, they needed to look to the future. The company collaborated with Bugatti motorcars and manufactured a boot or trunk in yellow cowhide to match the inaugural Bugatti Royale. Hermès also fashioned an accompanying bag. There were further joint ventures with the likes of architect Corbusier and notable interior designers.

The 1920s and 1930s proved to be a time of incredible expansion for the company. In 1922, Hermès launched their first ever publicly marketed line of leather handbags for women. Emile created this first collection himself, having been inspired by his wife who had complained about not being able to find a bag to her liking. In 1925, the first range of travel bags was launched,

THE NEXT GENERATION   19

encompassing the new 'zip' technology which, as the well-to-do across the world began to travel more for leisure, hit the zeitgeist with perfect timing. Nineteen-twenty-five also saw the creation of Hermès first ready-to-wear garment for men in the form of a leather golf jacket. The House of Hermès then introduced a capsule jewellery collection, including wrist watches. From the 1930s onwards, Hermès employed Swiss watchmaker Universal Genève as the brand's exclusive designer of time pieces, producing a line of men's watches in 18 karat gold or stainless steel and a range of women's Art Deco-style cuff watches in 18 karat gold or platinum. Both models contained dials signed either 'Hermès' or 'Hermès

LEFT: architect Corbusier
TOP: Bugatti Royale
ABOVE: 1943 Uni-Compax, Stainless-steel

THE FASHION ICONS — HERMÈS

Universal Genève' while the watch movements were signed 'Universal Genève S.A'. This partnership would last until the 1950s. The 1930s also saw the birth of what would become some of Hermès most recognisable items – such as the leather 'Sac a Depeches' bag in 1935. This was designed by Robert Dumas, a son-in-law of Emile's. Dumas designed a trapezoid shape with two triangular gussets, a cut-out flap, a handle and two side straps, launching the house into a new era of boldness and modernism. Twenty years on, the bag would become world famous as the 'Kelly bag' after Princess Grace of Monaco, formerly Hollywood film star Grace Kelly. By the end of the 1920s, Hermès was in the talks with the Neiman Marcus department store in New York City in order to secure a sales outlet in the US. Hermès were also utilising their leather techniques for fashion items. For instance, the studded leather collar originally made for a customer's bulldog was adapted to become a much-coveted fashion belt with the company officially launching their 'Collier de Chien' range in 1927.

ABOVE: Detail of a Collier de Chien belt
MAIN IMAGE: 'Sac a Depeches' bag

THE NEXT GENERATION 21

ABOVE RIGHT: Late 1920s Hermès adverts

ABOVE RIGHT: Late 1920s and 1930 Hermès adverts

THE NEXT GENERATION | 25

THE FASHION ICONS — HERMÈS

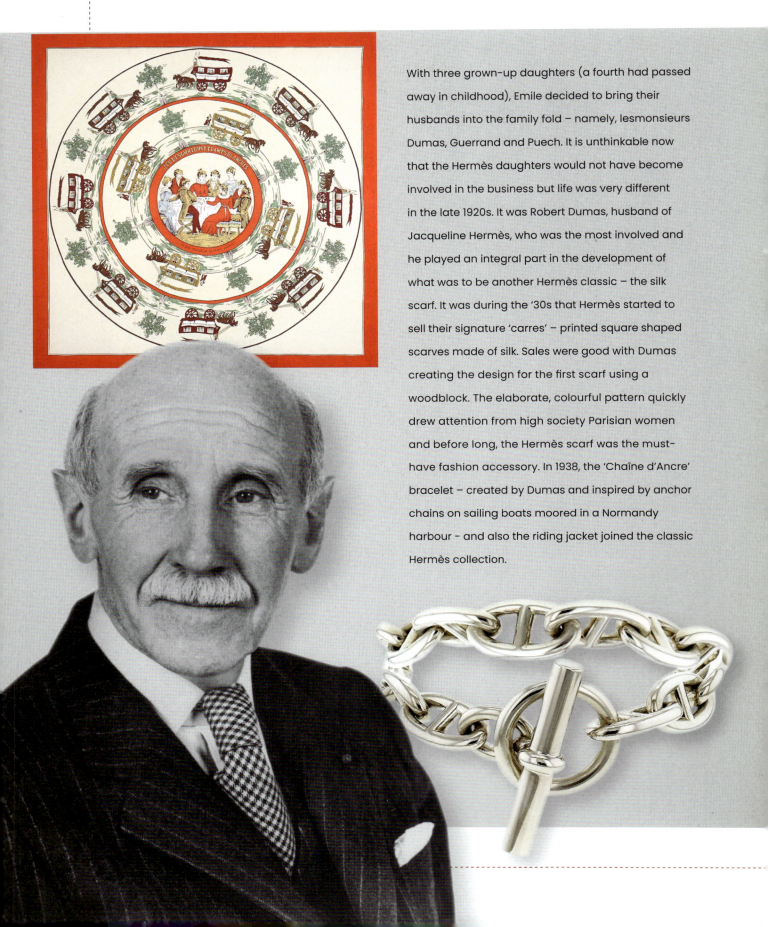

With three grown-up daughters (a fourth had passed away in childhood), Emile decided to bring their husbands into the family fold – namely, lesmonsieurs Dumas, Guerrand and Puech. It is unthinkable now that the Hermès daughters would not have become involved in the business but life was very different in the late 1920s. It was Robert Dumas, husband of Jacqueline Hermès, who was the most involved and he played an integral part in the development of what was to be another Hermès classic – the silk scarf. It was during the '30s that Hermès started to sell their signature 'carres' – printed square shaped scarves made of silk. Sales were good with Dumas creating the design for the first scarf using a woodblock. The elaborate, colourful pattern quickly drew attention from high society Parisian women and before long, the Hermès scarf was the must-have fashion accessory. In 1938, the 'Chaîne d'Ancre' bracelet – created by Dumas and inspired by anchor chains on sailing boats moored in a Normandy harbour - and also the riding jacket joined the classic Hermès collection.

THE NEXT GENERATION

LEFT: Robert Dumas & 'Chaîne d'Ancre' bracelet
TOP LEFT: Original design for the Scarf
ABOVE: Hermès scarf 'Cosmographia Universalis'

THE FASHION ICONS — HERMÈS

By this point, the company's designers began to draw inspirations from paintings, books, and objets d'art – in particular those collated by Emile Hermès who had been an avid collector since childhood. It was from this collection that Emile, in 1945, was inspired to create the now instantly recognisable corporate logo of a calèche and horses. Three years earlier the now famous orange Hermès gift boxes had come into circulation. During World War Two there was a shortage of cream-coloured cardboard. The supplier resorted to what supplies he had left. They happened to be orange. Voila! La Maison's legendary brand packaging was born with generations of orange-hued boxes following on since then.

Post-World War Two, saw an expansion in the range of gloves made by Hermès. In addition to their legendary sporting gloves, exquisite pairs for the theatre, the opera, for celebrities and even the Pope were crafted. It was around this period

TOP: Classic Hermès orange gift boxes
RIGHT: Vintage Hermès gloves
OPP. PAGE: Vintage Hermès advert, from the 1950s

THE NEXT GENERATION

THE FASHION ICONS — HERMÈS

that the famous revolving carousel display case took pride of place in the Hermès Rue de Faubourg store window. In 1949, the first Hermès neck-tie was launched by Dumas. The creation of ties by Hermès is an illustration of the house's entrepreneurial spirit. In Cannes, a number of gentlemen – having been refused entry to the casino – visited the neighbouring Hermès store in search of the requisite tie. This demand led the house starting to produce this silk accessory, which became an essential element of the Hermès men's wardrobe. 1949 also saw Hermès creating a special gift for Wallis, Duchess of Windsor. Some accounts say it was 'the Dook', as she called him, wishing to surprise her while others maintain it was a request from a house guest of the Windsors'.

Following an intricate design by Emile, a wooden barrow was customised, bound in black patent leather with gold plate trimmings and divided into three sections to house the Duchess' perfumes, gloves and flowers. The gift was so admired that Hermès received many requests for similar models. Emile, however, turned these down. The royal cadeau was a one-off!

A year later the first fragrance – the citrussy, spicy 'L'Eau d'Hermès– was launched, calling on the talents of another son-in-law, perfumier Jean Rene Guerrand, husband of Aline Hermès. In September 1951, at the age of 80, Emile passed away but the vision of his son-in-law successors meant that his beloved Hermès was in the best possible hands.

LEFT: 'L'Eau d'Hermès
ABOVE: Vintage Hermès Necktie, with Egypt design
RIGHT: Hermès perfumes on display today in Paris

THE FASHION ICONS   HERMÈS

EMILE'S TREASURES

Emile Hermès was just 12-years-old when his passion for collecting objets d'art, paintings, and books began. His first purchase is believed to have been made with the first two francs he earned as a tip and was an 80-year-old 'canne galant' – a gentleman's walking stick with a delicate parasol hidden within just in case a lady, while on a stroll with her gallant suitor, required protection from the sun. Collecting was to become a life-long passion. Many of his precious finds are now housed in the Emile Hermès museum which nestles on top of the brand's flagship store on Faubourg Saint-Honoré in Paris in a wood-panelled, temperature-controlled room which has been lovingly restored. The room was once Emile's study and before that the workrooms of his father, Charles-Émile Hermès. This ultra-exclusive museum is open only to Hermès' staff and selected stellar guests such as the late Elizabeth Taylor, Andy Warhol and Grace Kelly. It is Paris' best kept secret.

One of the most important objects is a painting by Alfred de Dreux, which portrays a waiting groom and a hitched carriage that inspired the brand's iconic logo which was introduced in the 1940s. Other highlights include a rocking horse which belonged to the son of Louis-Napoléon Bonaparte and a velvet saddle once owned by French statesman Adolphe Thiers. Everywhere you turn, there are horses. Paintings of horses, sculptures of horses, saddles – including hand-stitched saddles from the 1800s, bridles, carriages, spurs, whips, harnesses, and equine memorabilia. There are hundreds of other items, too. Pieces of furniture, cigarette cases, penknives, clocks, children's toys, glassware, crockery, clothing, jewellery, weapons, lithographs and thousands of books. The overriding theme is decidedly equestrian, however – the animal being at the heart of all Hermès creations.

The museum has been likened to an old curiosity shop - where toy models of royal carriages made from paper are positioned cheek-by-jowl with leather trunks made in the 18th century. The original 'Hermès Fastening' which resembles a kind of silver snake is also displayed. It is a reflection of the company's history and legacy, serving as a constant source of influence for Hermès designers. Every Tuesday, the maison's artisans are invited to visit the museum for inspiration. For the same purpose it is also frequented by Hermès' designers for accessories, ready-to-wear and crystal ware.

RIGHT: Rooftop of the flagship store on Faubourg Saint-Honoré in Paris

EMILE'S TREASURES 33

THE FASHION ICONS — HERMÈS

DAWN OF THE DUMAS DYNASTY

'My first love'

Robert Dumas on the Hermès scarf

On the death of his father-in-law, Robert Dumas became CEO of Hermès, co-operating closely with his perfumier brother-in-law, Jean Rene Guarrand. Dumas was to be in charge of the brand for almost three decades. More artistic but less gregarious than his late father-in-law, Dumas was mainly interested in new design with his focus being the Hermès scarf which he referred to as his 'first love.' So enamoured was he of 'les carres' that it was on his instruction that they began to be flown from the stores' rooftops like flags. Nine of the company's 10 best-selling scarves, including 1957's Brides de Gala (Gala Bridles, the all-time best-seller) and 1963's Astrologie (a favourite with fashion designers), were made on Robert Dumas's watch. These two designs – the ceremonial gravity of leather bridles and the overhead soaring of the spheres – symbolised the dynamic of Hermès. Earth and air.

In 1956, Hermès received publicity that turned out to be absolutely priceless. It was already known that the newly married Princess Grace of Monaco, former film star Grace Kelly, was a fan of the Hermès 'Sac-

ABOVE: Brides de Gala & Astrologie Hermès scarves
RIGHT: Prince Rainier of Monaco and American actress Grace Kelly, 1956

DAWN OF THE DUMAS DYNASTY

a-Depeches' handbag which had been launched 20 years earlier. She had been photographed with one of the bags when her engagement to Prince Rainier was announced, then she was pictured using the bag to shield her pregnant belly from the paparazzi. The image became extremely popular all over the world and was on the front cover of numerous magazines. The public renamed it the 'Kelly bag' and the purse began to grow in popularity throughout the world, giving the company much more exposure. The Princess led a very high-profile life and greatly influenced the fashion choices of well-to-do ladies and high-profile women in Hollywood. Although Hermès was already a well-known brand, having a bag named after the iconic actress and Princess helped its reputation grow and evolve into something new, giving the fashion house huge publicity. From then on, Hermès became extremely popular due to the iconic Kelly bag and even more women wanted to get their hands on one. They were all interested in looking like the Princess of Monaco and carrying Hermès in order to show their status and wealth. The Princess of Monaco had two favourite Hermès Kelly bags, both made with crocodile skin and in the stunning colours of dark brown and navy blue. Her love of these bags helped to make the crocodile skin design extremely popular in Hollywood, even more so than it had already been. Thousands of women dreamed of obtaining a crocodile skin Kelly bag of their own. They are still known as 'Kelly bags' to this day and the manufacturing process is also the same. Making the luxurious 'Kelly' takes extreme dedication and skill. Each individual bag is made by only one craftsman, which takes around 18 hours to put together. The bag is crafted with the most expensive skins and leathers available. The lining in the Kelly bag is made from goat skin and then the rest of the bag is made of durable leather with stunning grains and patterns that give each bag a distinct look.

Princess Grace was also instrumental in giving the Hermès scarf her seal of royal approval. In 1959, she was pictured boarding Aristotle Onassis' yacht with her arm in a sling after what was reported to be a particularly nasty wasp sting. Said sling just happened to be fashioned from a Hermès carre – the Deo Juvante Monaco silk square which had been issued in 1957/58.

ABOVE: Vintage crocodile skin Kelly bag
RIGHT: Princess Grace, boards Aristotle Onassis' yacht with the famous sling

DAWN OF THE DUMAS DYNASTY 37

ABOVE: Hermès Deo Juvante Monaco silk square
ABOVE RIGHT: Caparaçons de la France et de l'Inde detail
RIGHT: Sammy Davis Jr.

for bespoke orders, one Henri Manault, recalled SDJ's somewhat delayed reaction to the custom-made piece.

'*We met again four years later. He must have been pleased with the cabinet because, thanking me, he kissed me on the cheeks.*'

The late 1950s also saw the Hermès design team looking east. India was the inspiration for the name of a Hermès women's coat, Calcutta, and the Caparaçons de la France et de l'Inde silk scarf (a Philippe Ledoux design) paid dual homage to the sumptuous attire created for both horse and elephant.

Sammy Davis Jnr was another superstar of the time who frequented Hermès. During the 1960s, this ultimate showman commissioned a special kind of case to take with him on tour – a portable drinks cabinet, no less. It was made from black crocodile skin with a red leather interior which had been fashioned to hold wine, bourbon, mixers, a silver-gilt mess cup and a sandwich box. It's creator, the Hermès go-to artisan

THE FASHION ICONS — HERMÈS

window displays of the Faubourg Saint-Honoré store. Annie, who worked at the company between 1926 and 1970, was a Hermès legend, responsible for the stores award-winning window art and bringing the Hermès range of goods to life.

'To succeed in my line of business,' she famously said, 'you need to let rip with your imagination'.

Such was her attention to detail that when designing a stable tableaux for a window, she would spread horse manure over the floor for real, live sparrows to peck at!

A fourth generation Hermès joined the family firm in 1964 when Jean-Louis Dumas, son of Robert Dumas and Jacqueline Hermès, joined the luxury house. A year later, Emile Hermès' grandson Patrick Guerrand and trusted designer Henri d'Origny explored new horizons in Hermès' designs for men with the Hermès Sport label. The new ready-to-wear department offered bold interpretations of classic Hermès. In 1967, Hungarian-born stylist Catherine Karolyi joined the Hermès family in the professional sense. That

Further highlights from Robert Dumas' tenure included the hiring of of Leïla Menchari, a graduate of the Beaux-Arts of Tunis and Paris, at the beginning of the 1960s. She joined Annie Beaumel in designing the

TOP: French fashion designer Guy Laroche drapes fabric around Leila Menchari, before Hermès
ABOVE: H Belt, designed by Catherine Karolyi

same year, she created the first women's ready-to-wear collection for Hermès. Until 1980, she designed accessories – some of which became classics, like the famous H belt buckle.

Several new Hermès stores were opened during the 1960s and 1970s but there were fears the company was beginning to stagnate. Although Robert Dumas had been a safe, responsible pair of hands at the tiller of the good ship Hermès, with the luxurious brand becoming a household name, by the 1970s sales were starting to slow with ateliers having less and less to make. In 1971, Robert's son, Jean-Louis, then aged 33, was appointed CEO and Artistic Director of the company. Slowly he began to breathe new life into the house. One of his first moves was to launch the first issue of 'Le Monde d'Hermès' in 1973. More of a journal than a magazine, this publication was created in 1973 in Germany under the name Die Welt von Hermès, with Le Monde d'Hermès emerging in France two years later. Now translated into more than 10 languages, Le Monde d'Hermès is distributed throughout the world and also available in digital and podcast form.

Robert Dumas never officially retired. He passed away in 1978. The next chairman of Hermès? Jean-Louis Dumas, founder Thierry's great, great grandson.

RIGHT: Jean-Louis Dumas, early 1980s

THE FASHION ICONS — HERMÈS

LE SCARF

Hermès' 'les carres' (scarves) are so intrinsically chic, so sartorially stylish they have become totally integrated into French culture. Initially made from the finest imported Chinese silk, the first carrés or 'square scarves' were twice as strong as any other silk scarf on the market at the time, and by far the most versatile. Not only could the wearer fashion it around her neck, tie it to her saddle or handbag, she could use it for more demanding tasks – such as Princess Grace Kelly of Monaco utilising her Hermès scarf as a chic sling when she injured her arm in the late 1950s.

Since Robert Dumas's first scarf design in 1937 – his 'Jeu des Omnibus et Dames Blanches' using woodblock and inspired by an antique board game from Emile Hermès personal collection, Hermès has employed a number of renowned artists to create the nine new designs traditionally featured each new season. These include Kermit Oliver, a one-time mail man from Texas who is considered one of the greatest living American painters and the only US citizen to ever design for Hermès; Persian born artist Ugo Gattoni who has been with Hermès since 2012; Zoe Pauwels, a modern artist who has produced over 20 iconic scarves; Cathy Latham who has produced some of the most popular designs over the years including 'Les Cles', 'Washingtons Carriage', and 'Ferronnerie' to name just three of her 54 creations; and the late Hugo Grygkar, known as the 'Father of Hermès designs'. He created Hermès scarves for 15 years until his death in 1959, including the famous 'Brides de Cala' model famously worn by Sophia Loren.

ABOVE: Kermit Oliver with his children; Ugo Gattoni
ABOVE RIGHT: Cathy Latham's designs Les Cles & Ferronnerie

In all, over 2,000 designs have been created by Hermès since 1937, many of which have become limited edition re-releases of old designs. Others have been phased out to make way for new designs, making each scarf a valuable investment piece. Hermès hires artists to hand-design each scarf individually. Historically, designs have gone from traditional horse motifs to whimsical illustrations and just about everything in between. The scarves are so beautifully-designed, they are often framed and displayed as artwork. Once the design is complete, it is sent to a factory in France, where it is individually screen-printed – the design having being carefully designed onto the screen for printing. This process takes many hours. The result is a wearable work of art that tells the story of its artisans, and carries the legacy of the brand.

Each Hermès scarf, with its colourful and refined designs, tells a story – fantasy tales, abstracts and representations of the natural world. The house has around 50 freelance artists designing new scarves at any time, with the aim of creating 20 new designs each year. More than just an accessory, Hermès scarves are also, in their own way, socially responsible. Limited editions are often produced to support local non-profit organisations, which may deal with agendas concerning women's and children's rights, preserving the environment, protecting endangered species, and supporting art.

The silk used to make a Hermès scarf is derived from the cocoons of up to 300 Mulberry moths. This is the amount required for the 450 metres of finest silk yarn of which each individual scarf is made. Originally the silk was sourced from China but today Hermès possesses its own silkworm plantation in Brazil. One scarf can take up to 18 months to complete, making it one of the most meticulously-crafted accessories in the world. On average, each scarf has 27 distinct colours. It takes roughly 750 hours alone to engrave the screens for printing – one screen per

THE FASHION ICONS — HERMÈS

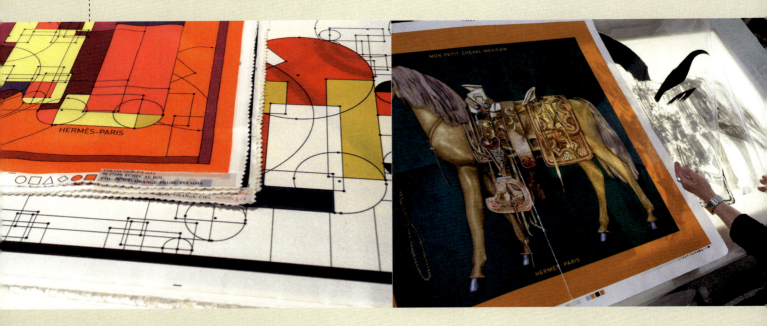

single colour. Manufacturing methods may have evolved since the first scarf was produced in 1937 but high-quality traditional craftsmanship remains standard. The Hermès scarf factory is situated in Pierre-Benite, near Lyon, known as the capital of silk in France. In the printing department, bolts of silk are fixed on immense tables measuring more than 100 meters long. The printer places a silk screen frame corresponding to one colour and one particular design, and applies the appropriate dye. The colours employed call for a variety of utensils worthy of a great chef. The assemblage of pigments under heat allows for the composition of 38 primary colours which, skillfully mixed, produce an infinite range of hues and shades. These steps are repeated as many times as the number of frames required to arrive at the final pattern. Depending on its complexity, 24 to 70 applications may be required. Once printed, the bank of silk is put to dry above the tables for the entire day. Later it is washed, dried, ironed and cut. Typically, each square measures 90cm x 90cm size and weighs approximately 65grams. The hems on the scarf's four borders are hand-rolled and hand-stitched.

Les carres have long been a favourite with the rich and famous. In addition to Princess Grace, the likes of Audrey Hepburn, Liz Taylor, Jacky O and Queen Elizabeth II were often seen sporting one - the latter notably to secure her hair while out with her horses. Italian superstar Sophia Loren is a fan while French actresses Catherine Deneuve and Brigitte Bardot have worn them since the 1960s as a bandana or headscarf, and more recently, Madonna used one as a halter top while Rihanna modelled a scarf as a bikini top. More traditionally, there are a variety of ways to wear Hermès scarves as headwear – it just takes a little imagination. Folded up, rolled up, loose with a triangle to the front or knotted around the neck, head, wrist and waist. . . the choice is yours.

ABOVE & RIGHT: Various production processes of the Hermès scarf

LE SCARF 45

THE FASHION ICONS — HERMÈS

It is possible to purchase a new Hermès scarf from one of their many stores or outlets, or, of course, from their website (www.Hermès.com). However vintage and limited-edition scarves are in great demand – but just how does one tell if they are authentic? Here are a few tips...

* Chose a reputable dealer or outlet such as www.vestiairecollective.com; www.sothebys.com; www.Hermèsscarf.co.uk; www.uk.thevintagebar.com; www.onlineonly.christies.com

* The hems should be hand-rolled, facing upwards, using thread that matches exactly the rest of the scarf.

* Print and colours should be clear, vibrant and incredibly detailed.

* All writing should be clear with a 'grave' accent (going downhill) on the 'e' of Hermès.

* There should be a copyright circled 'c' by the Hermès branding.

* The artist's name should be almost always included, often quite subtly, as part of the design, unless it is a very early design. The Hermès branding can sometimes be quite difficult – and fun – to find.

* Only the earliest scarves have the caleche (horse and carriage) logo printed on them.

* The care label should only be in French or English, unless the scarf is post-2018, and sewed into the corner with a couple of stitches - the thick thread exactly matching the rest of the scarf.

* Any scarf with an orange card label and orange plastic seal is fake.

* The scarf should measure 90cm square and weigh over 63g.

* The box should have a textured feeling with a narrow, well-printed black border and information printed on the inside. It should be relatively dull rather than a bright orangey colour. An authentic Hermès box is worth £25 on its own.

* Any doubts? Check every detail of your scarf against the equivalents advertised on other reputable sites.

RIGHT: A Hermès double-sided scarf, with a design created by French cartoonist Ugo Bienvenu

THE FASHION ICONS　HERMÈS

JEAN LOUIS & HIS LEGACY

'Time is our greatest weapon'

Jean Louis Dumas

As a young man, Jean Louis, one of the 17 cousins who made up the fifth generation of Hermès la famille, seemed unwilling to live and breath Hermès the fashion house. Born in Paris in 1938, he and his siblings were brought up in the culture of luxury, their family shops selling the famed handbags and scarves. But well-read and well versed in the arts, Jean Louis wanted to see the world. He did his national service in Algeria, studied law and political science, travelled the hippy route – Iran, Afghanistan and Nepal – in a Citroën 2CV, and drummed across Europe with a jazz ensemble. Then he spent a year taking the Bloomingdale store's buyer training programme in New York. But genes will out and in 1964, he finally joined the family firm becoming head of manufacturing. His love and respect for the craft never diminished.

'The world is divided into two,' he said. *'Those who know how to use tools and those who do not.'*

He became managing director in 1971. Then, to his surprise, the family voted him chairman after his father's death in 1978. When Jean Louis took over the reins of the company, it was regarded as stuffy and old-school rather than exciting and fashion-forward. Forbes magazine reported that there was not enough work to keep the crafts people and artisans busy - especially in the leather-working atelier above the store. Financial consultants suggested that the company close the atelier and hire outsiders to do the work— dismantling the heart and soul of the house, in effect. For Dumas, this simply wasn't an option. Instead, he looked to the future, much as his grandfather Émile-Maurice once had, and saw a re-imagined, global Hermès. A modern Hermès.

While Jean Louis was against accelerating Hermès' trademark slow hand-working of leather goods, especially when it came to the weeks spent in selecting the skins and the stitching of items, he wanted younger customers. Many more of them, too. He consulted a friend who worked at an advertising agency and asked what he should do.

'Hermès isn't for anybody considered a trendsetter,' came the reply.

It was clear a new vision and image was required and soon – more in the vein of the outrageous photoshoot

RIGHT: Jean-Louis and Rena Dumas-Hermès oversee the construction of the first standalone Hermès boutique in New York

THE FASHION ICONS HERMÈS

that Helmut Newton did for Vogue magazine in 1976, when, having called the Hermès store in the Faubourg St Honoré, *'the most luxurious sex shop in the world'*, he put an overtly sexual slant on the equine merchandise. The long-established Kelly bag suddenly became available in bright ostrich skins and in 1979, Dumas launched an advertising campaign, put up in Paris overnight, that pictured hip young Parisians wearing Hermès scarves with jeans—a look so radically 'high-low' the whole house of Hermès protested, an uproar that lasted days.

'The idea is always the same at Hermès,' Jean Louis commented. *'To make tradition live by shaking it up.'*

He recognized that both fashion and retail had changed, and if Hermès was to survive without compromise it had to reposition its products and make them relevant to more walks of life. Dumas expanded the Hermès profile by investing, usually at 35 percent, in companies that shared the Hermès ethic of No Compromise—companies like Leica optics and Jean Paul Gaultier's couture. He expanded the Hermès product line by buying entire companies that he believed in (eg, the London bootmaker John Lobb) and that made sense within the context of Hermès's new Art of Living department - Puiforcat silver and Saint-Louis crystal, for example. And he expanded the Hermès global presence with a steady increase in the number of boutiques and stand-alone stores, making few mistakes in a well-researched strategy of growth

The head of the US store Neiman Marcus said that Dumas *'revolutionised the market for Hermès by repositioning the products without changing the quality'*. He widened his market to Asia and the Americas, while closing franchise outlets and reclaiming distribution rights.

LEFT: Portrait of Helmut Newton and two models
ABOVE: Bright ostrich Kelly bags

THE FASHION ICONS　HERMÈS

'We have enough money to finance our own growth,' he said with optimism.

He was right to be so sanguine. It was in the 1980s that an idea of his was truly touched with genius. On a late-night flight from Paris to London in 1983, he found himself sat in First Class next to model, actress and singer Jane Birkin. She was carrying her signature wicker basket to hold her personal essentials. As she placed her straw bag in the overhead compartment, all the contents spilled out in front of Dumas, including her Hermès diary. Dumas assisted as she scrambled to collect her things. He joked that she needed a handbag with pockets. The actress replied that the day Hermès made a large everyday bag that could hold all the items a busy working mother carried, she would give up her signature oversized basket in its favour. The actress then explained how hard it was to find a spacious, secure, and stylish bag she liked. It was a light-bulb moment for Jean Louis. Incorporating feedback from Birkin, he drew the very first sketches of the Birkin bag on an airplane sickness bag. One year later, in 1984, the first Birkin bag was released. Its roomy interior made it an ideal jet-set option, and the lock meant it could be securely carried closed during travel. The clean lines, minimalist style, and casual flair perfectly captured Birkin's personal style. The rest is haute-couture history.

From 1982 to 1989, Hermès sales grew from $82 million to $446.4 million. New core, purpose-built

JEAN LOUIS AND HIS LEGACY

LEFT: Jane Birkin with her wicker basket
ABOVE: A Birkin Bag

THE FASHION ICONS | HERMÈS

ABOVE: Pantin workshops
RIGHT: Craftsman working in the Saddle Workshop

workshops were erected in 1991 in the Parisian suburb of Pantin. The leather workshops moved from the first floor of 24 rue Faubourg Saint-Honoré to Pantin, just outside Paris. The architecture of the new site offered a bright and spacious workspace for the artisans. Hermès were known for taking care of their people.

'We are like peasants working the land to yield fruit,' was one of Jean Louis' favourite sayings. 'The way the grandfathers of our grandfathers did.'

This was a sentiment he taken from his mother, Jacqueline, and it expressed both the sense of stewardship each Hermès generation felt – and still feel - towards the firm and also the simple dignity inherent in work done by hands with tools—the awls, mallets, needles, knives, and stones that populate the workbench of every Hermès artisan, each of whom received a training of five years. Hermès was - and continues to be different - from other luxury brands in that it is not so much a design identity as it is a culture, a rarefied world with its own values and ways of working. Retired workers do not leave the company but join its Club des Anciens—'the ancients'—which meets for monthly lunches and yearly trips and is a living library of company history and wisdom. The ancients are as much Hermès as the Hermès 'family' members, who even with advanced degrees in other fields may find themselves moving back towards their natural home – leather, silk, and the saddle stitch. In 1987, Hermès celebrated its 150th anniversary with a memorable fireworks display over the Pont-Neuf bridge in Paris. This event launched the first annual theme in a tradition that has been perpetuated ever since to nourish all forms of creativity with a shared source of inspiration.

THE FASHION ICONS | HERMÈS

Jean-Louis was not afraid to take chances when it came to the hiring of key design staff. In 1980, he gave 19-year-old Eric Bergère a senior job straight out of fashion school. In 1988, minimalist Creative Director of menswear Véronique Nichanian came on board, two years later Pierre Hardy took over women's shoes and jewellery while the hire of the esoteric Martin Margiela, engaged in 1997 for ready-to-wear, surprised many in the fashion world.

The first years of the noughties saw Jean Louis Dumas making his last hires, and they were important ones. In 2003, when the press-phobic Margiela decided not to renew his contract with Hermès, wanting to devote himself to his own line, Dumas again surprised the industry, by hiring Jean Paul Gaultier—bad-boy couturier, costumer of Madonna, and out-there showman. And Gaultier, who'd turned down many offers to design for other houses, surprised himself by wanting the job. Dumas had asked him for suggestions about who could take Margiela's place.

'I threw out a few names,' Gaultier recalls, *'but finally when I got home, I said to myself, "Me. I would love to do it". It's a house that allows for great creative freedom with no limits. My mother used to wear Calèche, and through the scent, Hermès was in my childhood memory. That's why I play with the Hermès codes, giving them a twist.'*

LEFT: Jean Paul Gaultier
ABOVE: Hermès Calèche

THE FASHION ICONS HERMÈS

JEAN LOUIS AND HIS LEGACY

The fragrance department - despite the success of the classic Calèche and other scents such as Équipage, Amazone, and 24 Faubourg— was the one Hermès division that underperformed through much of the 1990s. In Jean-Claude Ellena, hired in 2004, the company found its 'nose'. Ellena created the Hermèssences line — lighter, more ethereal mixes which proved very popular, especially with the young. With Jean-Louis Dumas still at the helm, Hermès developed across the world with the opening of numerous stores, each of which ingeniously combined the saddler's identity with local culture. Among these international stores, several Maisons Hermès were inaugurated - on Madison Avenue in New York in 2000; in Tokyo in 2001 in a building made of glass bricks; and in Dosan Park, Seoul in South Korea in 2006. Hermès also launched an e-commerce website in the United States in 2002, then another in France three years later.

ABOVE: Hermès Tokyo
LEFT TOP: Hermès Madison Avenue
LEFT BOTTOM: Hermès Seoul

In 2005, aged 67, Dumas began to loosen the reins and relinquish responsibilities. It was during this time of quiet transition that Hermès suffered the loudest, and possibly worst, publicity in its history. It has been dubbed a 'crash' moment but was really an unfortunate misunderstanding. On June 14 2005, US legend Oprah Winfrey and friends arrived at 24 Faubourg at 6:45 p.m. and were told the store was closed. This was true. Hermès closes at 6:30 p.m. But on this particular evening, because the staff was preparing for a fashion show, the store still looked open.

'The doors were not locked,' Winfrey later said on her television show. 'There was much discussion among the staff about whether or not to let me in. That's what was embarrassing.'

Newspapers and the Internet whipped the incident up into a frenzy. Hate mail poured into Hermès. The family was mortified. Dumas himself, had he been in better health, would have taken a flight to meet Winfrey, to explain that Hermès never closes its doors to anyone. In his place, Robert Chavez, the president and CEO of Hermès USA appeared on Winfrey's show to say how sorry the company was. She accepted the apology.

'What is the future of Hermès?' Dumas once answered this question with a single word – 'Idea'. In early 2006, when Dumas announced he would be retiring, Hermès found itself facing that future.

ABOVE: Hermès advert from the 2000's
LEFT: Oprah Winfrey

A GUIDE TO THE MOST-WANTED, LIMITED-EDITION HERMÈS BIRKINS

What happens when one of the world's most exclusive bags becomes even more exclusive? Hermès produces only a limited quantity of its iconic Birkin bag each year, making the maison's special editions, released every few years, incredibly expensive and extremely difficult to source. Created from start-to-finish by one craftsman, these handbags come in an array of materials and colours, and demand has never been higher. These deeply coveted, limited-edition styles range from uniquely utilitarian designs to dramatic pieces made in collaboration with renowned designers such as Jean Paul Gaultier.

THE SHADOW BIRKIN

At once dramatic yet understated, the Shadow Birkin was first introduced in 2009 by famed French designer Jean Paul Gaultier, Hermès's creative director from 2003 to 2010. A decade later, Hermès re-released the bag in limited numbers. For the Shadow, Gaultier sought to create a trompe-l'œil effect through the illusion of a top flat and sangles (ie, the name of the strap that originally held saddles on the backs of horses), shown casually strewn. In reality, the design is a raised impression, making it the only Birkin to stray from the traditional structure.

THE CLUB BIRKIN

One of the sportiest designs from the house of Hermès, the Club Birkin was first produced in 2012. Similar to the 2017 Touch Birkin, the Club often showcases exotic materials in its signature pair of vertical stripes. Yet, like the later Sunrise Rainbow model, colour-blocking is key. Therefore, the Club always includes a contrasting centre panel.

THE GHILLIES BIRKIN

One of Hermès's most coveted and hard-to-find designs is the Ghillies, which is distinguished by its decorative trim. Introduced in 2012, the Ghillies was an extension of the 'haute bijouterie' jewellery collection produced in 2011 by Pierre Hardy, artistic director of jewellery at Hermès. The design is inspired by a Scottish men's dress shoe of the same name, which has perforations known as 'broguing' which help the shoe dry more efficiently after outdoor activity. Hardy drew from his own heritage and adapted it into something stylish and functional — the brogue translated into a women's bag, making it even more feminine and detailed.

THE TOUCH BIRKIN

Released in 2017, the Touch is Hermès's answer to collectors looking for a hint of exotic material on their bags. This style is available in a variety of jewel tones and features a leather body with an alligator or crocodile top flap. Occasionally, other parts of the bag are also highlighted by pops of exotic leather. While collectors often prefer to wear their Birkins open for easy access to what's inside, the Touch best presents its exceptional details when worn closed.

THE TRESSAGE BIRKIN

Bags from Hermès's Tressage, or 'braided,' collection are defined by their panels of multicoloured woven leather. The Birkin iteration was introduced in 2018 and only produced in three colourways. It comes exclusively in 30 and 35cm sizes.

THE FAUBOURG BIRKIN

One of Hermès's 'Holy Grail' bags, the Faubourg Birkin was first introduced in a very limited edition at the end of 2019. Originally making its debut in two colourways, brown and navy, Hermès has now dazzled collectors with a new version in a beton-type hue. The style of the bag is modelled after the façade of the Hermès flagship at 24 Rue du Faubourg Saint-Honoré and comes complete with orange awnings and a clochette designed after the house's iconic orange shopping bag. The Faubourg is the first Birkin Bag ever to be crafted in a 20 cm size, and it is finished with sleek Sellier stitching, a detail typically reserved for Kelly bags and very uncommon for Birkin bags.

SUNRISE AND SUNSET BIRKIN

First produced in 2020, the Sunrise and Sunset Rainbows are exclusive Birkins finished with sellier stitching. Generally reserved for the house's Kelly handbags, 'sellier' refers to the visible outside stitching which gives the bag a crisper, more structured shape. An eye-catching design that is perfect for summer, the Sunset handbag's colour-blocked effect combines Lime, Rose Confetti, Terre Battue, and Sesame, while the Sunset version features Cricot, Bleu Agate, Magnolia & Rouge Casaque coloured Epsom leather.

THE CARGO BIRKIN

Making its debut in 2020, the Cargo Birkin is another of Hermès' most recent limited-edition styles. Crafted in lightweight canvas and sporting five outer pockets, it is the most functional Birkin to date. At its conception in 1981, the Birkin bag was celebrated for its practicality in comparison to other bags at the time. Nearly 40 years later, Hermès has cleverly played on that original principle of practicality with the addition of something for those busy mornings on the go — a coffee cup holder.

THE SO BLACK BIRKIN

The So Black collection, currently one of the most desirable on the market, was not always as coveted as it is today. Designed by Jean Paul Gaultier, the black hardware effect is created thanks to a special PVD (physical vapour deposition) coating. When it was first released in 2010, it was swiftly pulled from distribution because the delicate nature of the hardware made consumers wary that it was impractical. Of course, this only served to attract collectors. Offered in either Calf Box Leather or Matte Crocodile, the exotic iteration is significantly more valuable and arguably the most sought-after Hermès bag.

THE 3 IN 1 BIRKIN

The 3-in-1 Birkin, which first graced the runway at Paris Fashion Week in spring 2021, is defined by versatility. The distinctive 'pochette' can be attached to the handbag and used as a compartment, or removed and carried as a standalone clutch. When detached from the pochette, the bag becomes a handy tote. At once capacious and compact, this clever reinvention of the classic Birkin silhouette is a must-have for seamless transitions from day to evening.

THE FASHION ICONS — HERMÈS

FAMILY VALUES

'I knew that my heart was with Hermès, but I always thought I was not good enough'

Pascale Mussard, niece of Jean Louis Dumas

Who would take the place of Jean Louis Dumas? Three individuals as it turned out. With the approval of the Hermès board, company veteran Patrick Thomas who had first joined the house in 1989 became the new CEO while Jean Louis's son, Pierre Alexis, and his niece, Pascale Mussard, were made co-artistic directors.

'This is a family company with a long-term vision,' announced Thomas. 'There will be no revolution.'

For Pierre Alexis, the House of Hermès was stamped through his DNA like letters through a stick of seaside rock.

'One very important feeling for me is the feeling of humility,' he announced. *'That came about very early, that I never took Hermès for granted. It was a house – our house – and a highly respected institution.'*

By 1976, aged 10, Pierre Alexis had already been chomping at the creative bit and asking to learn the famous saddle stitch. *'It's not really about the stitch,'* he recalled some years later. *'It's about being aware of the sense of touch, being able to stitch with your eyes closed, being able to represent yourself and the object you're making in space, being able to listen to what your hands tell you. These are fundamental acts which built our civilization. When I was able to control my hands, I was so proud.'*

Pierre Alexis had graduated with a degree in visual arts from Brown University in the US, where

RIGHT: Patrick Thomas with Pierre-Alexis Dumas, in the leather goods workshops in Pantin
ABOVE: Pascale Mussard

FAMILY VALUES

fellow students sometimes confused Hermès with Aramis, a popular men's fragrance in the 80s. A misunderstanding that surprised him yet he also understood the confusion. Hermès the brand may have been around for close to 200 years yet it maintained a youthful, fresh outlook because it was constantly changing and reinventing itself while also paying homage to its illustrious history. Immediately upon starting at the company in 1991, Pierre Alexis joined the creative committee for Saint Louis crystal and Puilforcat silver - both high end brands acquired by the Hermès group some years earlier.

After a year, Dumas headed up the group's operations in Hong Kong, Taiwan and China, a position he would hold for five years before completing the same role in the company's United Kingdom division. He returned to his creative roots in the noughties, having become director of silks in 2002. He continued in the position until his father's retirement.

'My father never told me he wanted me to be creative director,' Pierre Alexis revealed. *'I had to fight for it and prove by the results of my work that I was worth it. My job is to keep the strong creativity of Hermès alive. To nourish the rigour and the vision... to make these values vibrate. The core of Hermès today is the same is it was then - know-how. And today after almost 200 years of experience we have not only one set of expertise linked to working leathers, but also know-how in textiles, and in many, many other different métiers. So, what we have to now do is keep trying. We have to go back to work. We have to think of new ideas, new applications that confront our ability to fashion the material and which extend our ability to transform it.'*

From the very start of his tenure, Pierre Alexis signed off on every Hermès product – and continues to do so to this day. He has a natural affinity and love for the company's iconic scarves.

Like her cousin, Pascale Mussard, who is descended from the Guerrand branch of the family, could not remember a time when the House of Hermès had not figured in her life.

'The key of my parents' apartment was the same key as all the offices and the safe of Hermès,' she was to say. *'My uncles could come every day at any hour.'*

After school she would go to the Hermès upstairs atelier to watch the leather workers or to play on the terrace. After studying law and obtaining a degree in business, she began at Hermès as a fabric buyer in 1978, when her uncle Jean Louis took over. Not that it had been a given. It was company policy never to employ a Hermès just through family connections alone.

'I knew that my heart was with Hermès, but I always thought I was not good enough. When Jean-Louis asked me to join, I was astonished. He said to me, "You know every corner at Hermès, you know every person". He helped a lot of people to bloom.'

In critiquing a window Pascale had dressed, one she was proud of, Jean Louis Dumas taught her an important lesson in the unique Hermès allure.

'He said, "It's not a good window—everything is too Hermès. You are like a good pupil, and a window is not about that. You have to make a reaction. You have to surprise. You have to astonish yourself. Be always on a wire, a thread".'

Pascale asked her uncle what was the USP of Hermès? What made it unique amongst other high-end brands? Jean Louis quoted his father Robert's words — Hermès was, and is, different because they made a product that could be repaired.

'It's so simple - and it's not so simple,' Pascale has said. 'Think that you can repair something because you know how to repair it and why it has been damaged. You have the hands. Think that you can repair it because you want to keep it. And think that you can repair it because you want to give it to someone else. I think it's right. It's what Hermès is about.'

Pierre Alexis also followed his father's example as he moved forward.

'My father was always anxious,' he recalled. 'He had stage fright, convinced that when everything was prepared, at the greatest events, it will not work. And it was always a success. I understand today that that attitude is a wise one. If you just say everything is OK, you're not taking risks. The brand is going to be affected by that. Slowly it's going to become banal.'

Dumas took charge of all the silk, textile accessories, and ready-to-wear with Mussard's responsibilities being leather, jewellery, and non-textile accessories.

'Pierre is very abstract,' she said. 'He loves paintings, he wants to be a painter, he loves things flat. I love three dimensions. I love objects. And so we are very complementary.'

The cousins were also very much aesthetically in sync. Like Dumas' mother, Rena, Mussard's father had been an architect. Having both grown up with modernist values, Pierre Louis and Pascale found common ground in a love of clean shapes with strong energy. From the beginning of their joint tenure, they wanted the company to grow slim and fit with a light – but not too light - touch. As cousins, they had known each other forever, understanding immediately and innately what was right for the brand and what wasn't.

'We've got to remain true to ourselves,' says Dumas, 'but we've got to change constantly. And it's that tension which is at the heart of Hermès.'

In 2008, Pierre Alexis created Fondation d'Entreprise Hermès - a new dimension to its patronage policy and philanthropic commitment with the tagline,

'What we do creates who we are.' In keeping with the artisanal and humanist values of the family company, the aim of the foundation being to work mainly in the fields of creation, the transmission of know-how, the preservation of the planet and solidarity through its own support programmes, both in France and abroad. Two years later, 'Le Petit Workshop' was created under the leadership of Pascale Mussard, adopting a unique approach within the house, that of creation in reverse. Starting with unused materials from Hermès manufactures, artisans and designers were to give free rein to their inventiveness to create unique and unexpected objects, building on the exceptional knowledge of the house.

Axel Dumas, another cousin of Pierre and a sixth-generation member of the Hermès-Dumas clan was appointed Executive Chairman in 2014. He had joined the family business

ABOVE: Exhibition by Turkish artist Nil Yalter, part of the Fondation d'entreprise Hermès, La Verriere, Brussels, Belgium

THE FASHION ICONS — HERMÈS

11 years earlier as an auditor, becoming CEO of its jewellery division in 2006, and the CEO of its leather goods division in 2008. He was appointed as chief operating officer and joint CEO of the company alongside Patrick Thomas in June 2012, succeeding Thomas as CEO of the entire maison in February 2014. Axel strengthened the dynamic growth of the group with the inauguration of the fifth Maison Hermès in Shanghai in 2014 and the opening of many more stores worldwide.

It was this trinity of both Dumas' cousins and Pascale Mussard that held sway over the family business until 2018 when the latter left her post as principal of 'le petit workshop'. However, it is believed she remains on the Hermès board. Compared with its contemporaries, Hermès is unique in that it firmly remains a family run firm with 66.7% of its shares held by the family-owned group.

'Hermès has grown out of a family culture with a set of values that we all believe in,' says Pierre-Alexis. *'I am convinced it would disappear if the family dimension was taken away or diluted. You know, there have been a lot of very good, small restaurants in Paris that have been bought by big chains over the years, usually in the name of better management. But somehow their clients have stopped going, because they have lost their souls.'*

ABOVE: Veronique Nichanlan, Axel Dumas, Robert Chavez, Pierre-Alexis Dumas, Henri-Louis Bauer, at the opening of Hermès Beverly Hills Boutique, 2013

FAMILY VALUES 73

THE FASHION ICONS HERMÈS

HERMÈS BY NUMBERS

9
Each seasonal collection of scarves consists of nine prints

20
The number of seconds between Hermès selling a silk scarf across the globe

19,700
The approximate number of people employed by Hermès worldwide

600
The cost in pounds for a small dog's Hermès raincoat

311
The number of Hermès stores worldwide

100
The percentage of Hermès leather goods made in France

24
The number on the door of the iconic Rue de Faubourg Hermès store in Paris

16
The number of heirs to the Hermès fortune

100 PLUS
The number of Birkins said to be owned by Victoria Beckham

13,000
The amount of items in Emile Hermès' treasure trove of a museum

3
The Dumas are France's third richest family

HERMÈS BY NUMBERS

6 — Is the amount of years for the longest waiting list for a Birkin bag

202,000 — The approximate number of products repaired in Hermès workshops each year

48 — Hours are required for one artisan to create a single Birkin bag

200 — The number of Hermès Birkin and Kelly bags owned by influencer Jamie Chua from Singapore. She had her closet enlarged to make room for them all. Jamie is said to have the

65 — The number of grams each Hermès scarf weighs

57 — The number of fragrances and colognes launched by Hermès

10 — The percentage that neck ties make up of Hermès sales

7 — The number of cardboard manufacturers making the iconic orange Hermès packaging

45 — The number of nations boasting Hermès outlets

16 — The total artisanal métiers feeding the creativity of the house.

54 — There are 54 Hermès production and training sites in France

100,100 — The price in British pounds paid for Jane Birkin's bag which she sold on eBay in 2011 in order to raise funds to benefit earthquake relief efforts in Japan

THE FASHION ICONS   HERMÈS

READY-TO-WEAR CREATIVE DESIGN

'I think people want to be more in style than in fashion'

Jean Louis Dumas

It was in the 1980s that the creative design of Hermès Women's ready-to-wear collections finally began to be taken seriously. At the dawn of the decade, Jean Louis hired young Milanese designer, Eric Bergère, who on taking on the role as head of RTW, declared that Hermès garments looked like they had been designed for *'very, very old women'*. Bergere radically modernised the label by making jackets out of frog and toad skins, jeans from ostrich skin, and covering shoes and handbags with its famous 'H' logo. Hermès executives credited him with waking up the company's fashion but he left in 1989 over strategy disagreements. He was replaced by Claude Brouet, long-time editor of fashion and beauty at France's Marie Claire magazine and who launched her first collection for autumn/winter 1989-90. It was Jean Louis' wish to develop a women's RTW collection that would not abandon Hermès's equestrian and silk looks, but would complement them with seasonal fashion colour, fabric and styling trends. While Brouet and her team achieved this, by the mid 1990s it was once again felt necessary to give the brand a shake-up in the RTW metier.

In April 1997 Belgian designer Martin Margiela was appointed new creative director of Hermès. Many wondered at the time how such an avant-garde, pioneering creative could have 'landed' at Hermès, and, in particular, what had prompted Jean Louis Dumas to make such an appointment. Margiela was no people pleaser, he wanted his work – tops made

ABOVE: Claude Brouet And Nicole Crassat. France, 1982
RIGHT: Martin Margiela, early 90's

READY-TO-WEAR CREATIVE DESIGN

THE FASHION ICONS — HERMÈS

of plastic bags, waistcoats made of broken plates, and dresses made from candles – to speak for itself. Just how would Margiela interpret the Hermès classics? It seems Jean Louis' daughter Sandrine played a part in the two men coming together. She had modelled for the Belgian designer several times in the 1990s in exchange for clothes. When asked by her father for a recommendation for Brouet's replacement, she immediately replied that Martin Margiela was the person. A single lunch was enough for both Margiela and Jean Louis to realise that they shared a common vision of fashion as synonymous with relaxation, comfort, quality and longevity. The 12 collections that followed under Margiela's direction

ABOVE & RIGHT: Martin Margiela for Hermès, Fall 1997 Ready to Wear Runway Show
FAR RIGHT: Vareuse blouse

READY-TO-WEAR CREATIVE DESIGN

from 1997 to 2003 were in perfect harmony with Hèrmes' past, as he made the style of the label his own. His creations were characterised by a simple, monochrome yet extremely refined look – classic luxury. They were very different to those he created for his own line yet the garments reflected these in subtle ways while also marrying well with Hermès. For instance, the use of Margiela's signature absolute white with the classic Hermès' burnt orange. Then there was his famous Vareuse blouse with a very

THE FASHION ICONS   HERMÈS

deep V-neck, one of the essential components of the modular look made of layers and overlaps that the Belgian designer created for the French house; the convertible trench coats; his evolution of the twin set to the triple set; the invention of the trikini... Margiela gave an undeniably new flavour to Hermès – some of which lives on to the present day in the form of the Losange scarf – a twist on the classic Hermès scarf, and the iconic Cape Cod watch, characterized by a long bracelet worn as a double loop on the wrist.

ABOVE: Cape Cod model luxury wristwatches
LEFT: Convertible trench coat
RIGHT: Losange scarf

READY-TO-WEAR CREATIVE DESIGN 81

82 | THE FASHION ICONS — HERMÈS

ABOVE & RIGHT: Martin Margiela for Hermès Fall 1998 Ready to Wear Fashion Show

READY-TO-WEAR CREATIVE DESIGN 83

THE FASHION ICONS   HERMÈS

ABOVE & RIGHT: Hermès Ready to Wear Fall/Winter 2001-2002 fashion show as part of the Paris Fashion Week on March 11, 2001 in Paris, France

READY-TO-WEAR CREATIVE DESIGN 85

86 | THE FASHION ICONS | HERMÈS

ABOVE & RIGHT: Spring 2003 Hermès show in Paris

READY-TO-WEAR CREATIVE DESIGN

THE FASHION ICONS   HERMÈS

Margiela left Hermès in 2003 to concentrate on his own label. In his place, his former boss - the flamboyant Jean Paul Gaultier who had famously created the conical bustier corset for Madonna - was appointed Creative Director. This was another Jean Louis hiring that raised eyebrows in the fashion world. Elegant, exquisite Hermès appeared to be an odd pairing for the rebellious and theatrical Gaultier. However, this juxtaposition proved an exciting partnership. Gaultier's tenure at Hermès, spanning from 2003 to 2010, was a period of exceptional creativity and design evolution. His collections for the brand were nothing short of

READY-TO-WEAR CREATIVE DESIGN

FAR LEFT: Jean Paul Gaultier 2002
ABOVE & ABOVE LEFT: Madonna's conical bustier corset

THE FASHION ICONS   HERMÈS

spectacular, as he seamlessly blended his avant-garde sensibilities with Hermès' rich heritage. Gaultier reimagined the brand's classic pieces, such as the iconic Kelly and Birkin bags, imbuing them with his signature touch, shrinking, for instance, the Kelly to a chic clutch and changing the proportions of the Birkin, most notably elongating its shape.

In addition to revolutionizing Hermès' accessories, Gaultier's vision extended to the brand's clothing lines. He pushed the boundaries of the Hermès aesthetic, introducing bold prints, unconventional materials, and sculptural silhouettes to the collections. Under his direction, Hermès became a trailblazer, captivating audiences with its daring yet sophisticated designs. For his first collection - autumn 2004 - he heavily featured equestrian themes with riding regalia and leather used in every possible way. It's clear that Gaultier's tenure at Hermès has been one of the highlights of his career.

'Hermès was a challenge for me because I was so punky. Maybe I did Hermès because my ex-assistant Martin Margiela did Hermès also. His collection was not Hermès at all and I remember seeing it and thinking that's great, it's fabulous, it's exactly what it needs to feel more modern but still respecting the code, bravo! But also, I saw what I would have done. So, then I saw Monsieur Dumas and he asked me to do it, at first I said no I cannot because I already have too many collections to produce, but then I thought, oh, why not? Martin did it very well, would I do it as well as him? Or better? No. I didn't do better, I did it my way.'

ABOVE: JPG's revision of the Birkin & Kelly bags
RIGHT: JPG's Kelly muff
OPP. PAGE: Autumn/Winter 2004-05, Paris fashion week

THE FASHION ICONS HERMÈS

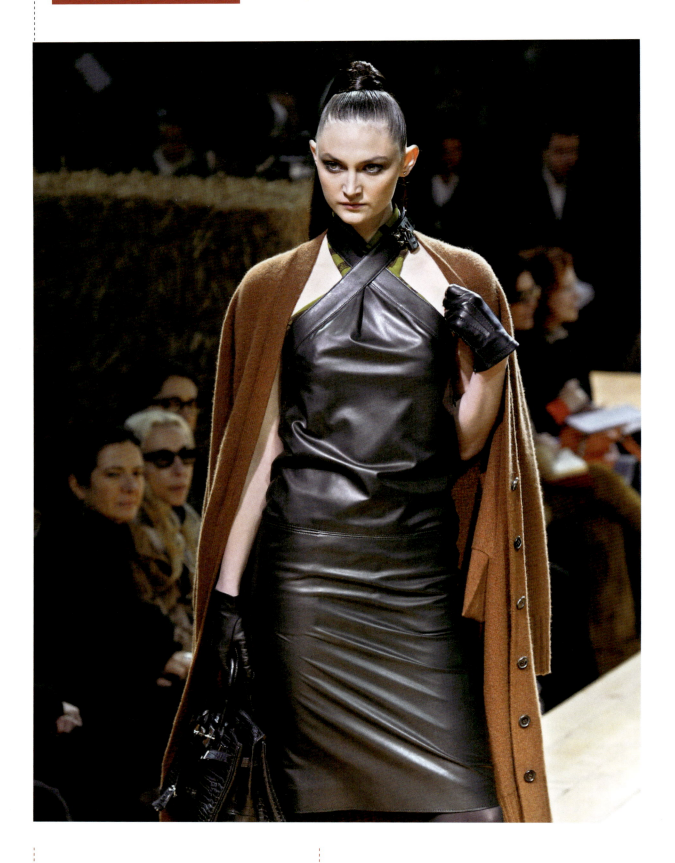

ABOVE & RIGHT: Autumn/Winter 2004-05 collections at the Paris fashion week

READY-TO-WEAR CREATIVE DESIGN

THE FASHION ICONS   HERMÈS

ABOVE & RIGHT: Spring-Summer 2005 Ready-to-wear Fashion show in Paris

READY-TO-WEAR CREATIVE DESIGN

THE FASHION ICONS | HERMÈS

ABOVE: Spring/Summer 2007 ready-to-wear collections in Paris

READY-TO-WEAR CREATIVE DESIGN 97

THE FASHION ICONS   HERMÈS

ABOVE: Autumn/Winter 2007/2008 ready-to-wear collection show in Paris

THE FASHION ICONS | HERMÈS

ABOVE: Models and Jean Paul Gaultier on the runway at Hermès' spring 2010 show at Halle Freyssinet

READY-TO-WEAR CREATIVE DESIGN 101

THE FASHION ICONS   HERMÈS

ABOVE & RIGHT: Spring/Summer 2011 ready-to-wear collection show on October 6, 2010 in Paris

THE FASHION ICONS | HERMÈS

ABOVE: Spring/Summer 2011 ready-to-wear collection show on October 6, 2010 in Paris

READY-TO-WEAR CREATIVE DESIGN

THE FASHION ICONS HERMÈS

MAIN IMAGE & RIGHT: Paris Womenswear Fashion Week Fall/Winter 2011 at Halle Freyssinet on March 10, 2010 in Paris

THE FASHION ICONS **HERMÈS**

READY-TO-WEAR CREATIVE DESIGN

Christophe Lemaire, former Creative Director of French sportswear brand Lacoste, took up the Hermès Women's RTW reins after Gaultier's departure due to Jean Paul desiring more creative freedom and wishing to concentrate on his own brand. Lemaire, was an unexpected and, to some, underwhelming appointee. The verdict of his first collection was mixed.

'Perhaps the collection suffered from too-muchness, a heaviness,' wrote Cathy Horyn in The New York Times. But others approved, including Suzy Menkes of the International Herald Tribune praised it as *'a fine effort for a first season'*. Another admirer was Virginie Mouzat, fashion director of the French daily newspaper Le Figaro. *'I loved it!'* she said. *'The quality is irreproachable. Simple cuts. Wonderful fabrics. Beautiful silks and leathers. Seasonless outfits. It isn't sexy, loud, or in your face, and for some people that can be boring. It's a very slow, discreet, low-key notion of luxury—more style than fashion.'*

As his Hermès journey continued, Lemaire's designs displayed a minimalist ease that were a marked change from the more flamboyant designs of his predecessor, Jean-Paul Gaultier.

Lemaire's were looks for women who preferred a less ostentatious, more classical approach to fashion.

'You have to think about the comfort, the functionality, the pockets, the way the clothes will age,' he said. *'The inside is as important as the outside. The extreme quality that you feel, rather than show, is extremely important.'*

LEFT: Christophe Lemaire
RIGHT: Hermès Autumn/Winter 2011-2012 ready-to-wear collection in Paris

THE FASHION ICONS | HERMÈS

ABOVE & RIGHT: Hermès Ready to Wear Spring / Summer 2012 show during Paris Fashion Week

READY-TO-WEAR CREATIVE DESIGN 111

ABOVE & RIGHT: Hermès fall 2011 show, designed by Christophe Lemaire

READY-TO-WEAR CREATIVE DESIGN 113

THE FASHION ICONS　HERMÈS

ABOVE & RIGHT: Hermès spring 2013 show

READY-TO-WEAR CREATIVE DESIGN

Lemaire's tenure was a time of quiet glamour and restrained quality – covetable coats and highly wearable separates combined with exquisite materials and colour palettes.

'I like clothes that suggest, rather than show, the body, and bring attention to a woman's wrists and neck. Straight lines. Big sleeves. Big pockets. Pure. Fluid. Quite geometric.'

Lemaire achieved a kind of breakthrough for Hermès – women's fashion that blended its rich heritage with an understated, uniquely Gallic mode of chic.

As Margiela and Gaultier had done, Lemaire left Hermès to work on his own fashion line. In 2014 – after four years at the helm – Nadège Vanhee Cybulski, formerly of Maison Margiela, Celine and New York brand The Row – was appointed new creative director of Hermès prêt-à-porter.

'I knew I wanted to work with her because she has three very important qualities: a genuine appreciation and understanding of craftsmanship. She has a modern and emancipated vision of women, and is able to work in a collaborative creative environment,' said CEO Axel Dumas on her appointment.

For Cybulsk the creative process began – and still begins – with colour which she feels offers input and insight into which materials to use and which forms

RIGHT: Spring/Summer 2014, Paris
OPP PAGE: Nadège Vanhee Cybulski

READY-TO-WEAR CREATIVE DESIGN 117

THE FASHION ICONS   HERMÈS

to build. Functionality and beauty are the objectives she pursues combined with a quiet, calm luxury. Movement is important, too.

'I like to challenge gravity and play with the way you cut a fabric,' she has said. 'The way you direct it. The straight grain has a more controlled attitude, whereas the bias cut is more feminine, it waits for its owner before taking its final shape—then it comes alive. It's very dynamic. The concept of playing is something that is definitely part of the Hermès' DNA. For example, when people think of a Hermès scarf, they probably think of iconic prints such as Grand Manège or Cavalcadour, which were created by Henri d'Origny. I like to take these heritage prints and deconstruct them, open the valves and bring in a bit of air. Create something a bit lighter and fresher.'

Cybulsk's creations are rich in artisanal heritage, with the attention to detail, quiet elegance and sublime use of house leather and fabrics. Hers is a modern definition of womenswear that is comfortable, functional and forward - with a few throw-back 1990s elements for good measure. The result is something both functional and sensuous but never overdone. More and more, she wants to know that her clothes are sustainably made. Vanhee-Cybulsk doesn't think she has all the answers but feels that the bigger the company is, the more altruistic it should be.

While Women's RTW has seen several creative directors come and go over the years, the men's metier has had just one. Veronique Nichanian has designed sophisticated men's 'clothing objects' for the company since 1988.

RIGHT: Spring/Summer 2014, Paris
OPP PAGE: Nadège Vanhee Cybulski

READY-TO-WEAR CREATIVE DESIGN

ABOVE & RIGHT: Hermès fall Fall/Winter 2023-2024

THE FASHION ICONS   HERMÈS

ABOVE & RIGHT: Hermès Ready to Wear Fall/Winter 2024-2025, Paris fashion week

READY-TO-WEAR CREATIVE DESIGN

THE FASHION ICONS — HERMÈS

'I am lucky to have been able to use the most exceptional materials for Hermès,' says Nichanian who has maintained a discreet personal profile during her time at the house. 'It is essential for me to work with the know-how of traditional craftsmanship, combined with the latest technological advances.'

Her very first collection for Hermès won her the City of Paris Grand Prix of Creative Art prize.

During her 35 years as artistic director of Hermès' men's universe – the longest tenure of any current creative director in Paris – she has entered the house's historic archive only twice. She is steadfast that her vision is one of forward movement – each collection, she insists, is about looking ahead, never back.

'We don't have the same materials, we don't have the same life. So we are always thinking: what is the classic of tomorrow?'

This attitude and her lengthy tenure at the brand, has made Nichanian an undeniable force with an innate understanding of Hermès and a fastidious approach to creating a garment, which can hinge on centimetres of cloth - 'a centimetre can change the entire cut of a pair of trousers'. At the centre of her approach is the belief that Hermès, while synonymous with Parisian luxury and craft, should nonetheless retain a feeling of joie de vivre.

RIGHT: Men ready-to-wear Autumn-Winter 2010-2011
MAIN IMAGE: Applause for Veronique Nichanian after the spring-summer 2006 Men's ready-to-wear collection show for Hermès

READY-TO-WEAR CREATIVE DESIGN

THE FASHION ICONS | HERMÈS

ABOVE: Mens ready-to-wear Fall/Winter 2024-2025

READY-TO-WEAR CREATIVE DESIGN

'I think fashion should be light and fun,' she says. *'I want to bring happiness to people – in the sensuality of the fabric, or the colour, or something that makes you say "wow".'*

Nichanian's approach is intuitive, usually beginning with a colour card, which she then talks over with her team.

'They know me very well,' she says. *'To their first ideas, I say, "yes", "no" or "why not? Let's try". It's a very open discussion.'*

When it comes to the show itself – where Nichanian works alongside the house's other métiers, such as footwear or accessories – she says she is like the conductor of an orchestra bringing everybody together.

Luckily, Jean-Louis Dumas, when he hired her, gave her complete creative freedom, a luxury she is still afforded today under his son, artistic director Pierre-Alexis Dumas.

'It's about freedom and passion. All my friends who are in fashion are jealous of me. If I don't want to do a jacket, I don't do a jacket. I think this is key to keeping the creativity and savoir-faire.'

The template for a Nichanian menswear collection is deceptively simple – the perfect balance between colour, texture and shape, and a refinement of the way these elements interplay with one another when the wearer is in movement. She insists that she never feels restrained by the rules of menswear and having to design primarily within a canon of archetypal garments.

'I think it's interesting to find the right proportions – there is a black sweater and then there is an ugly black sweater. There are so many different types of trousers, so many different details, it's a very wide world. People say, "Oh, you design menswear, it's so boring". But it's not. If I was bored, I would do something else.'

THE FASHION ICONS   HERMÈS

ABOVE & RIGHT: Menswear Spring/Summer 2020

ABOVE: Menswear Spring/Summer 2023

READY-TO-WEAR CREATIVE DESIGN

THE FASHION ICONS | HERMÈS

ABOVE & RIGHT: Menswear Fall-Winter 2023-2024

ICONIC HERMÈS

'It's not a bag, it's a Birkin'

Samantha Jones, Sex and the City

It's a no-brainer for the Birkin to head up the list of Hermès most iconic creations. Since its birth in 1984, the bag has graced the arms of some of the world's most glamorous and high-profile women – Madonna, Beyonce, Lady Gaga, Kim Kardashian, Rhianna and the late Jane Birkin, of course – and become the most wanted purse of all. The Birkin positively screams exclusivity, class, sartorial flair and Parisian chic. And the fact that the price tag reads like a telephone number and the wait for one is comparable with the length of a pregnancy makes it even more desirable. In 2018 a matte-white Niloticus crocodile Himalaya Birkin became the most expensive handbag ever sold when it was auctioned for HKD$2.98 million at Christie's auction house.

THE KELLY BAG

The Kelly bag's design was originally meant to carry a saddle or a pair of boots. In the 1930s, Hermès decided to revamp the design and named it the Sac à Courroies, becoming a favourite handbag of the maison's elegant customers. It was first associated with Grace Kelly after was photographed carrying it on the set of To Catch a Thief. Then a few years later, when she had become a Princess, she shielded her pregnant stomach with her purse. Each individual 'Kelly' takes 25 hours and 2,600 hand stitches to create.

THE SCARF

The very first Hermès scarf was introduced in 1937 and inspired by a woodblock drawing by Robert Dumas, one of the sons-in-law of Emile-Maurice Hermès. Over the years, the scarf has remained the most popular product of the house being favoured by Queen Elizabeth II, Grace Kelly (who famously used her Hermès scarf as a sling), Audrey Hepburn, Catherine Deneuve, and Sarah Jessica Parker, to name but a few.

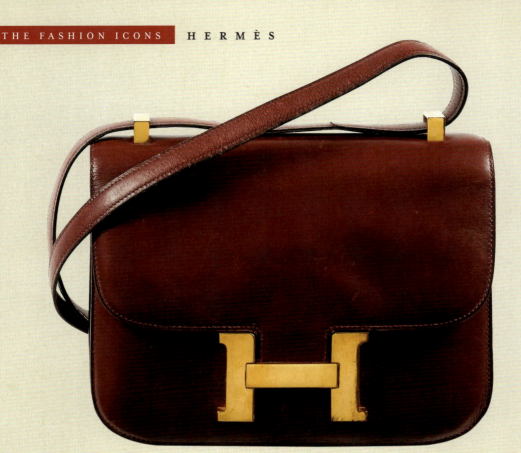

THE CONSTANCE BAG

The Constance was designed by in-house designer Catherine Chaillet who named the bag after her daughter. After it was introduced in 1959, it has become one of the brand's most loved bags. A flap bag, a large H acts as its clasp. The Constance is currently offered in four sizes: the micro, mini, 24 cm, and Elan. Fans of the design include Jacqueline Kennedy Onassis, Nicky Hilton Rothschild, and Diane Kruger.

THE CLIC CLAC BRACELET

Hermès makes plenty of enamel bracelets, but none compare to the popularity of the Clic Clac. The bracelet takes its name from the sound it makes when you toggle the clasp to take it on or off. The Clic Clac's design features the letter H in the centre as its clasp while being flanked by shiny, coloured enamel. It is available in three sizes as well as a more streamlined and more masculine version for men. There are about a hundred colours to choose from and three hardware options: silver, gold, and rose gold.

COLLIER DE CHIEN

Inspired by a dog collar, the Collier de Chien is one of Hermès' most popular leather bracelets. The Collier de Chien motif was born after the maison was commissioned to design a collar for a client's bulldog. The pyramid studs and O ring attracted several other dog owners in Paris, but it was only after couturière Marie Gerber had the idea to order it in a belt that it really took off. Today, the cuff is made in all kinds of leather with exotics such as crocodile and lizard as the most prized.

CONSTANCE BELT

The Hermès Constance belt is the ultimate as far as logo belts go. It's Hermès' unmistakable letter H that makes the belt. When worn properly, it can make any outfit look more elevated and adds beautiful shape. The beauty of Hermès' Constance belt comes from the fact that different style buckles and leather straps are completely interchangeable. Not only that, the straps are reversible with several different colour and leather combinations to choose from.

THE FASHION ICONS   HERMÈS

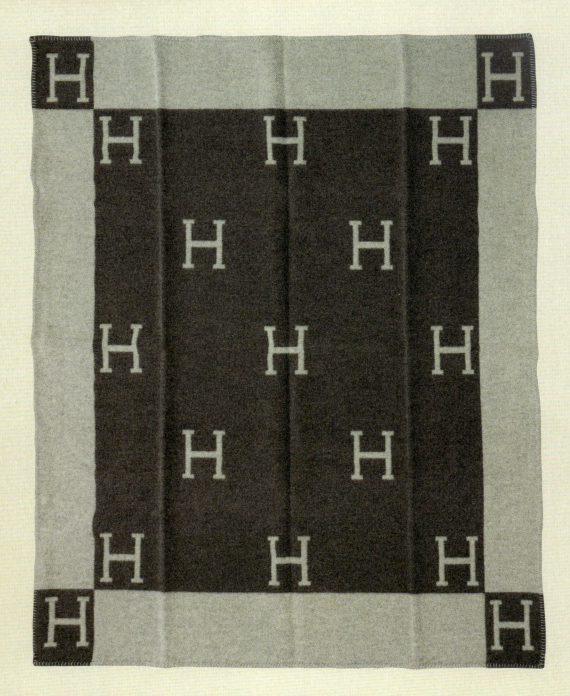

THE HERMÈS 'AVALON' BLANKET

The Hermès 'Avalon' blanket which debuted in 1988 has become the ultimate statement piece for the home. Sporting a signature pattern, the blanket is made in a sublime – not to mention soft – mix of merino wool and cashmere. It comes in a variety of colours and sizes – from a large throw down to a baby blanket.

THE ORAN SANDAL

Though a relatively new design, the Oran has become one of the maison's most iconic shoes. Released in 1997, the Oran was designed by Pierre Hardy for Hermès. The sandal can be characterized by its H-shaped vamp and the notable contrasting stitch detail. As is the custom with Hermès, the Oran has been made in the house's range of signature leathers and in several different colours but the black and the tan remain the most wanted.

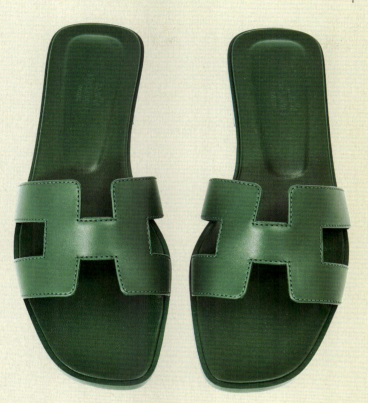

THE CAPE COD TIMEPIECE

The Cape Cod timepiece. It features all things signature to the house such as a leather strap, double tour bracelet, and chain motif. What makes the Cape Cod extra special is its understated elegance and ability to blend in perfectly with all manner of dress codes.

THE FASHION ICONS   HERMÈS

POST SCRIPT

At the time of writing, the House of Hermès is 187-years-old and there is no reason to suggest that it will not go on to celebrate its bi-centenary in 2037 – and beyond. Moving forward, refined excellence in all areas will continue to be the Hermès ethos coupled with an unerring ability to interpret the sartorial zeitgeist in its own inimitable way. A responsible company, Hermès strives to limit its impact on the world while respecting nature and the source of its exceptional materials. Transparency, security and the local dimension of supply chains are the subject of particular consideration. All over the world, the house's repair workshops preserve the sustainability of their objects, which develop a patina as they're passed on from one owner to the next. In 2022, over 202,000 Hermès products were restored, ensuring longevity. Meanwhile upcycling department 'Petit H' continues to take excess materials to create one-off or limited pieces. Upcycling ensures the unwanted materials remain in circulation rather than in a landfill. In addition, the maison has partnered with biotech company, MycoWorks, to produce a new animal-friendly leather alternative made from mushrooms. In late 2021, the company released its first bag – the Victoria bag – made using this new material. The eco leather plays a part in the house's ambitious plan to achieve net-zero emissions by 2050.